Lost in the Storm…

Poems by Jonathan Heidenreich

Jonathan Heidenreich

 www.trafford.com

North America & international
toll-free: 1 888 232 4444 (USA & Canada)
phone: 250 383 6864 ♦ fax: 812 355 4082

Lost in the Storm

Dedication

For Helen and Paul Demmer

Acknowledgments

My family
For your undying love and support,
Without you my words are without a soul

Joshua Stahl
For your support in all my endeavors
"Here's to hitting one into the lumber yard"

George Jaber
For giving me the chance to share my love of the Bard with others

William Shakespeare
From this student, to his hero

Thank you

Preface

The scroll of this age has unraveled her self to us. Her vacant valley of parchment lays pail with anticipation. It is our task as beings to scribe the page, and make whatever mark we so choose. For my own part I know no greater privilege than this, to leave behind a lineage of language. A literary fingerprint meant to connect with and inspire others. Therefore, confined within the binding of these pages lies my meager mark. This work you Hold within your fingers is not an obscure assortment of writings. Nor is this a memoir strewn with painted words and pretty phrases, lacking any hint of human center. But view this rather as a journey, across the landscape of the human heart. This is the journey of a poet, attempting to peer at him and life, through the looking glass of the pen.

My purpose in entitling this collection *"Lost in the Storm"* was to create for the reader a reoccurring theme. The theme being that life itself is a storm, filled with moments as fast and fleeting as the wind. Life, a pulsing tempest, overflowing with experiences that may touch us as gently as does the rain, or strike us as mightily as the lighting meets the earth. Deaths, rebirths, loves lost and won, are all seasonal storms that shape who we are. And be assured, though the thought of storms may conjure images of a fearful nature, there is such a thing as a beautiful storm. Our first kiss and our last, the thunder and its blasts, are all currents of air carving out who and what we are.

I hope you find fragments of yourself within these poems. A few of them I have made in personal dedication, to individuals who helped me to weather my own storms. I have included in this volume a eulogy, one I wrote and recited at the passing of my dearest inspiration, my grandmother.

Without her none of this would be possible. The rest remain as experiences, emotions, and passions that all that have ever lived, loved, or lost have surely felt. I promise you, these are not the cathartic ramblings of a ten-cent poet, but an exposition of the spirit…told by a 15-cent poet.

A lover's Interlude

You piloted the flame that engulfed my spirit,

Set the bait that ensnared my heart,

Laid the course my dreams would travel,

And through our smoke, found a spark,

Like the pattering of rain against the walls of mourning,

You washed the sadness from my brow,

Through your love I found my patience,

And all the joy the heaven's allow,

In my hands I have found your servant,

In my soul I have found your vessel,

In my eyes I have found your worship,

And in my heart a love majestic,

So fear I not the days of woe,

Nor the thorny paths of time that grow,

But bury me in this veil of love,

And die I never as the stars above.

A lover's song 2

The piety of patience has taught me to endure,
The nails of scorn,
And trails of thorns,
The world has promised sure

Though summer's eves may come and leave,
Their fragrance turned to frost,
Our loves incased, in my heart's vase,
Never to be lost

Though colors may corrode,
And paintings pass to dust,
Our passions shade will never fade,
In this, I do entrust

The notion of devotion resides within my core,
Wherein you have taken all forsaken,
And freely asked for more

I cannot touch with word or sound,
The love that my lone heart has found,
So here I stand your speechless serf,
                    Who with a kiss, shall prove his worth.

Lover's song

Let the thunder shake what it may,
Our love will stand another day,
Let monuments pay for their stones decay,
Our love will stand another day,
Though our mortal strings may tear and fray,
Our love will stand another day,
Though abrasive winds may haunt our paths,
And leave in disarray,
From this course I will not stray,
Our love will stand another day,
And when we are gone,
The world will say,
A love was here,
And here to stay

Maze of my own making

How cold is the air when it breaches our senses?
How sweet is the sound of painted promises?
How tailored is the art of misleading intentions?
How hindered is the heart when it meets it undoing?

You… who cast your silhouette over my soul

Clouding my reason, compromising my compassion, gauging your swaying hand over my own judgment, like a lord over his laborer

I lost myself to you, in a maze of my own making

Beauteous tyrant, you claimed what you could and left what you could not

So must I hate you? No, I could never move myself to hate you.

It is not in me to hate that which I have inhabited,

To hate those eyes that have marveled my own,

To hate the voice that has echoed through the very columns of my spirit.

If ever I could hate you, I must then hate that part of myself which cries out for you.

No, in its stead I will lay these passions to rest,

I will sleep, as I have before,

Dream, as I will again,

Wake, as I always have,

And breathe, as I do now, my heart's repetition keeping pace with the morning prior.

And above all live, as I have from my first breath, to the last I have yet to meet.

I will do all this, and I will not hate you.

But I will not love you

A Song for William

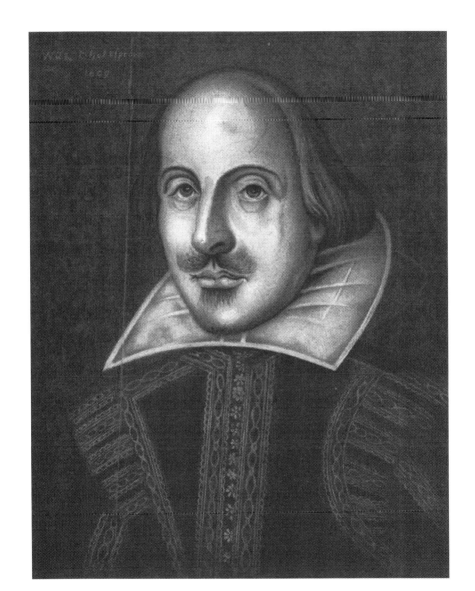

For Shylock's vengeance,

And Lear's disdain,
For Richard's immovable mark of Cain,

For Henry's triumphs,
And Hamlet's spite,
That ever I was born to read and recite,

For the fools of Arden,
And Iago's lies,
For the tears which fall from Ophelia's eyes,

For Titus's grief,
And Juliet's joy,
For the man that you've made from out of this boy,

For Macbeth's ambition,
And Priam's fall,
For the lifetime of language you've given us all,

For the winds of the Tempest,
And Othello the Moor,
For the blood that was spilt on the senate floor,

For Ado about nothings,
And Caesar's will,
For the songs that you've played at the point of your quill,

For the delight I derive on the night of the twelfth,
To all of your volumes which conquer my shelf,

For all of the worlds that you've turned into stages,
And all of the feelings you've formed into pages,

For the words, words, words you have left us to hear,
I thank you my hero, William Shakespeare

Adversity's song

O weary life, O endless strife,
I drink from forth your chalice,
And with each drop, of crimson slop,
I burry all your malice

I beg no cease, nor sweet release,
From out your titans grip,
For I have seen, your powers wean,
No doubt your hold will slip

Horrible and most grotesque,
Are the intentions you express,
But still I'll press you to my chest,
And take it all in loving jest

Your wrath resides within a glance,
To dissuade those from taking chance,
Yet against your winds I'll force a dance,
And in these revels find romance

I'll cauterize the ancient wounds,
That has made men much stronger swoon,
Then close the door unto your tomb,
                    And upon her steps play a tune

Always

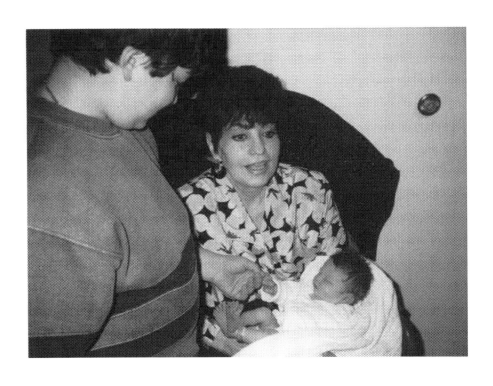

Looking back across the time we've spent,
The years we've had,
O' The things you've meant,

Through every test,
Through every trial,
You kept us loved,
You made us smile,

Though pains arose,
And joy delayed,
Never did your smile fade,

Though you'll go to god's command,
Never will you leave my hand,

Over this I will not weep,
For always in my heart you'll keep,

So many miles left to go,
But where they lead, time will show,
No matter where,
No matter when,
Your eyes will I see again,

You are the shelter we have known,
You are the love that you have shown,

Now rest your heart upon this cloud,
I pray to god I've made you proud,

And in my prayers I hope you see me,
Always will you be my Mimi

By Her Grandson for Helen

Aristotle's eye

As I gazed into the sky I saw,
My eyes imprisoned by Leo's paw,

When Saturn's Scepter graced my palm,
I felt my fears turn thus to calm,

I saw the sea Orion races,
Filled with Greek and Roman faces,

From out this starry pageant breaks,
The light that Mount Olympus makes,

O what ancient scenes are there to see?
Upon the heels of Mercury,

When all the dreams that were…now be,
As all the gods now smile on me,

And when I die, be this my plea,
To make my tomb antiquity

Common Interlude

The dwindling flame of our soul's candle dims in the ever incasing night.

The winding road of our life's path approaches swiftly upon its end.

Time willingly moves on and we find ourselves ever the more acquainted with the vulnerability that keeps us from our potential.

The fears that keep us from our sleep,

The doubts that keep us from our endeavors,

The pains that keep us from our promises,

And the lies that keep us from ourselves.

What fragile creatures we are made when the fear of our inward flaws surfacing rises to our temples height.

Such we are,
Such we have been,
Such we will remain.

Guardian

How could you be cold, when I have showered you with warmth?

How could you feel the rain, when I have sheltered you in storms?

Why do you fear the mountain, when I have taught you to climb?

Don't disdain the path, when your hands are in mine,

How can you fear the darkness, when I have been your light?

Why wish for the morning, when I come in the night,

Don't await the end, when each day is a beginning,

Let no silence be found, in my heart there is singing,

Hold our memories dear, but let this be said…

I'm found not in the past, but what lies ahead,

With roads left to walk and years left to battle,

Look not to the sky, in your heart I will travel,

When this climb meets its end, I'll carry you home,

With love left to share and worlds left to know,

So open your eyes, and begin down this path,

Your guardians watching, from here… to the last

I am

I am a blue eyed son with a heritage as deep as the Mediterranean.

I am the dream of my ancestors manifested in flesh and bone.

I am the heart that beats along with the battle drums of my people.

I am an image lost in time.

I am the blood that flowed through the veins of my father.

I am a chance taken by my mother.

I am a fingerprint of those who came before me.

I am the fire that burns in the soul of Vesuvius.

I am the hills of Cervinara, refusing to bend to the wrath of the elements.

I am the fields of Avellino, ever roaming, never taming.

I am the warriors of my people, never breaking, never fleeting.

I am loyalty in human form.

I am the tears that fall from St Gennaro's eyes.

I am the struggle of my people's existence.

I am the soil of Naples, whose roots grows deep and flourishes with life.

My lungs are filled with the sweet air of Sorrento.

My dreams rise from the ashes of Pompeii.

I am the child of a culture.

I am.

I'd cross the world

I'd cross the rivers, shores, and streams…Until your likeness left my dreams.

I cross the mountain peeks and paths, to here your voice call me at last.

I'd cross each railway, trail, and track, until our hearts had brought us back.

I'd cross the highlands, hills, and mounts, until my love did thee account.

I'd cross the plateaus, steppes, and plains, for no region rivals love's terrain.

I'd trek all roads that you had traveled, until my mind becomes unraveled.

I'd cross the tundra's of my soul, until your love had me whole.

I'd cross the winds, and storms, and skies, if only to behold your eyes.

No place on earth would call me home, until your lips had met my own.

I'd cross the world a thousand times, until that day I'd made you mine.

Lost in the storm

Memories have turned to winds that blow without remorse,
I've heard such roars, in times before, but never with such force,

And with each blast, I see the past, each image turned to thunder,
As I fight the tides, which quickly rise, and try to pull me under,

Each drop of rain has left a stain, that's painted all my soul,
The colors of a man in pain, who bids the thunders roll,

There is no hiding, from the clouds colliding, their faces dark and frightening,
But through these eyes, I fear no skies, and call upon the lightening,

Hurricanes of haunting dreams do crash against my core,
But I will never, fear such weather, no matter what's in store,

I know in length, with faith and strength, I'll see my angel's form,
Until that day, with love I'll stay, Lost within the storm.

The Lover, the warrior, and the Poet

The lover utilizes the heart,
The warrior his strength,
And the Poet his mind,

Forces though separate in their conception, remain all three alike in action.
Each one must account the other; each of them drawing from the same well.

The lover utilizes his heart, but must have a tongue to convey his love,
and a wit to conceive his love, and a mind to conjure words of such sweet
fragrance as to win his object to his love.

The warrior relies on his strength, but must first draw from his heart to face
his opposition, to withstand the trials of conflict, and surpass his opponent
by all means of his strength.

The poet employs the mind, yet must the poet find refuge in his strength to
walk the strange and endless corridors of the mind, boundless in fears and
doubt, endless in self reproof, through these pathways must the poet remain
strong, so as to mend his sorrows into sonnets of beauty and self reflection.

The Lover, the Warrior, and the Poet.
Three separate outlets of the human spirit, yet each eclipse the other.

Each alike, each different

Ode

Let old age come,
And senses numb,
Though my mind may turn a-miss,
My love is found,
Through time abound,
In the beauty of your kiss,
Though winds may roar,
And tides may rise,
And flowers turn to flies,
My refuge calls,
Not in these walls,
But only in your eyes,

Though words have hung upon your ruby lips,
As tapestries of art,
There is no sound,
O so profound,
As the beating of your heart,

Though life may offer blows and tears,
None have moved me such,
As the love that lingers,
In your fingers,
And the feeling of your touch,

Though my life will one day end,
And my soul one day ascend,
And my blood,
Though thick as mud,
Will surely turn to sand,
I fear this not,
My body's rot,
For I once held your hand,

You are my sun,
You are my eve,
You are the faith which I believe,
Though storms may call,
Fear not my fall, For I will never leave

Philosopher's eye

All fall so that they may rise,
Reach for the stars so we may touch the skies,
Smile with our hearts, so we may weep with our eyes,
Dream of the heavens while we dwell with the flies,

Live in the moment to honor the past,
Fear not the future, nor the clouds that it casts,

Draw strength from submission, and patience from pain,
Find victory through vision and lose all disdain,

Days are tailored too short to sit back,
And let your ambitions fall short of attack,

Hold on just tight enough to let go,
When those that you love need distance to grow,

But let not their hearts slip free of your hold,
Nor let their love crack from its mold,

Our dreams carry on long after we die,
Such it is seen through the philosopher's eye

The Poet's Forest

His wishful eyes, which watch the skies,
For signs of seasons starting,
Will with a tear, for each New Year,
Weep upon their parting.

Quarries of contemplation lie vast across his soul,
To which effect, he then must trek,
To make his spirit whole.

Raindrops turn to crystal dreams which dance across the wind,
And in this chase, for which they race,
A path that never ends.

Tales of lives and lovers lost coat his mourning mind,
And like the cost, of winter's frost,
Stays frozen to the vine.

Through this weird and winding wood,
Must our poet loot,
To find the tree of truth and see,
How deep doth grow its root.

There is a world

There is a world outside the plans we make,
The lies we tell,
The smiles we fake,
An hourglass of time and chance,
Whose grains of sand with hope, advance,
As history's pages swiftly fall,
The written script of time and all,
Though winds may rough our portly sail,
The pass of time will never fail

There is a world outside of us,
No formal range, nor lines to trust,
Paths evasive, roads unknown,
Where seldom through the light doth shone,
Where droughts erode, and fires wind,
Yet still the grass will grow with time

There is a world outside of me,
O what fruit is born from such a tree?
What brilliant minds did scribe the page?
And held their hour upon the stage,
Who made what meager mark they could,
Upon this stage such men once stood

There is a world outside our petty thoughts,
Its discourse held speaks that of loss,
There is a world of wonder made,
From whose thunder never fades,

There is a time, there is a place,
There is a world of earth and space

There is a world outside us all,
Remains it still though the stars may fall

Truth's a seasoned soldier

Truth is a seasoned soldier…
Wanted when he is missing and wished gone when he arrives.

His sword stays sheathed only so long…
For when it is revealed, it cuts without remorse.

His course is everlasting,

His intent-noble,

His opposition-many,

But his person-unscathed

What defines a man?

Is it the roads he's traveled?
Or the lives he's touched?
The sacrifices made?
Or not so much?
The blood he's shed?
The tears withheld?
The time he's spent?
Or the pains he's felt?
The friends he's lost?
Or the ones he's gained?
The scars he's caused?
Or the ones sustained?
The lessons he's learned?
Or the ones he's taught?
The battles won?
Or never fought?
Is it the dreams he's dreamt but left to chance?
Or moments seized without a glance?
Is it the obstacles he's faced?
Or the goals he's set?
Or just to live without regret?
Is it the love he's felt?
Or just to play the cards he's dealt?
The years he's spent or the time he's lost?
Or the need to win at any cost?

Is Man a mark you leave behind?
Or just another state of mind?

Where did you go?

When the tasks of life weighed heavy on my soul,
Where did you go?
When the fangs of fear took their toll,
Where did you go?
When the world's wonders lost their grandeur,
When timeless songs lost their rapture,
When there was still time to capture,
Where did you go?
When my strength's solidity lost its mold,
Where did you go?
When the grips of doubt took their hold,
Where did you go?
When passion's heat sub missed to cold,
Where did you go?
When the sounds of smiles became that of old,
Where did you go?
When all eyes where left wanting,
Where did you go?
As fires raged daunting,
Where did you go?
When words were left unspoken,
Where did you go?
When hearts were cleft and broken,
Where did you go?

Minutes, seconds, days, and hours…perhaps this time was never ours.
I feel the morning closing in; perhaps we'll meet one day again.
Though our time was poorly spent, and my heart now sorely bent,

Promise me…Remember me…Wherever you have went.

In Your Arms

When life had lost its simple charms,

I fell into your arms,

When cast alone into the unknown,

I fell into your arms

When crossroads came to sway my aim,

I fell into your arms,

Never need to cope with loss of hope,

I fell into your arms,

When words alone left love un-shown,

I fell into your arms,

When tears, like toys, where used for joys,

I fell into your arms,

Though I know, that I must go, into a world not free from harms,

I will shake this earth, with love and mirth,

Until I reach your arms,

And when I'm there, as love must share…

I will hold you in MY arms.

In remembrance: Eulogy

Thank you all for coming, knowing Mimi this would have made her world to see all of you here. "Leslie does my Hair look ok?" yes, Mimi. How could the world's most beautiful grandmother be so self-conscious?

This entire week has been life altering to say the least. I find myself lost in a storm of memories, some good, some difficult, and so many incredible. I stand here as a testament of the love, nurturing, compassion, and joy that was Helen Demmer. Is it truly possible to condense in a few minutes, the life of someone as special as my grandmother? A woman who meant so very much to all who came in contact with her? Is it possible to confine the years, memories, senses, and emotions that Helen created for all of us, into a simple eulogy?

When faced with the task my mind immediately escaped to so many Yesterdays. I see an 8 year old Blondie at the mall with his grandparents, his Pop Pop sitting on the bench outside of Macy's, while the boy's petit grandmother, against the laws of nature, laps him in walks around century three mall. I joyfully recall shopping sprees at the "Dollar Tree" store. I'm taken back to sleepovers in the den of my grandparent's house, sugar free Jell-O and egg beaters on a tray, and in the morning carnation instant breakfast with a silly straw, not to skip a beat. A house surrounded with ceramic angels. I remember putting into a cup on the living room floor as my grandfather stood behind me correcting my stance. I see myself nailing the back of a Pitt mug, as my grandmother cheers me on. I'm taken back to my childhood paradise. Our life saw many changes, some good and some difficult. But no matter the hour, no matter the circumstance, Mimi would be there.

Storms large and small, come what may, Mimi was there. When thinking of the hope she always provided, several instances come to mind. When my parents were separating, and my whole world seemed to be tearing at the seams, my grandmother held me in the game room where we had shared so many sleepovers. As I cried rocking in her arms, she stroked my head and assured me "everything is gonna be ok, sweet pea, everything will be ok". Fast forward to the passing of my grandfather, I stood by his casket, again tears in place of words raining from me, and who was there to hold me yet again, but Mimi. There she was, An 80 lb peanut of a woman holding the weight of a sobbing 200 lb baby. But in that instance she held up not only my balance, but my heart, my faith, and my hope.

On her last day I remember rushing over from school after receiving the call that our Mimi wasn't doing well, and she may not make it. I immediately broke down in my aunts arms, fearing the death of my childhood. When I saw my grandmother she was tired, she had been a fighter in every sense of the word. As I sat by her bed, I took her hand in mine, and sobbing I looked her in the eyes and told her how much I loved her. She awoke and turned to me, even though she was drained and near the end she was as beautiful as she always was. I had so many fears and so much to hold on to. As I clinched her hand I told myself "you can't let go, I won't let go, I'll never let go" but in that very moment her eyes met with mine and in them I saw the world, as perfect and wonderful as god had ever made it. She smiled with all her might, and without hesitation I pressed her hand against my lips. "I love you" I cried, without enough strength in me to stand. In a moment that will stay with me until the end of my life, a dying woman took my hand and raised it to her lips. Even in her last hours she was comforting me, SHE was comforting me.

Again in the heart of an 8 year old Blondie I heard her say "everything is gonna be alright sweet pea, everything is gonna be alright".
("Always" poem)
I love you Mimi.

Author's Final Thought

Time is a tale that's meant to be told,

And the future, a fiction that's yet to unfold,

The present provides the patience, we pray,

To dare to dream another day,

And alas the past is a shadow we cast,

On memories and moments we thought were our last,

But no time like now is ever so rare,

So give not the past, nor the future a care

About the Author

Jonathan Heidenreich is a poet, actor, and education major. He dedicates his life to the study and teaching of Shakespeare's folio. He lives with his family and three dogs in the South Hills of Pittsburgh, Pennsylvania.